ISAAC ASIMOV

THE ACHIEVERS

ISAAC ASIMOV

Scientist and Storyteller

Ellen Erlanger

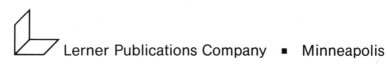

Lerner Publications Company ■ Minneapolis

Special thanks to Dennis Lien for the loan of his September 1941 *Astounding Science Fiction.*

LIBRARY OF CONGRESS CATALOGING-IN-PUBLICATION DATA

Erlanger, Ellen.
Isaac Asimov — scientist and storyteller.

(The Achievers)
Summary: Relates the life story of the "born storyteller" who came to America from Russia at the age of three and grew up to become one of the world's most prolific writers of science fiction and non-fiction.
1. Asimov, Isaac, 1920-   —Biography—Juvenile literature. 2. Authors, American—20th century—Biography—Juvenile literature. 3. Scientists—United States—Biography—Juvenile literature. [1. Asimov, Isaac, 1920-   .
2. Authors, American. 3. Russian Americans—Biography]
I. Title. II. Series.
PS3551.S5Z58   1986   813'.54 [B] [92]   86-10675
ISBN 0-8225-0482-0 (lib. bdg.)

Manufactured in the United States of America

2   3   4   5   6   7   8   9   10   96   95   94   93   92   91   90   89   88   87

For my brother Bill...

ISAAC ASIMOV
Scientist and Storyteller

Every morning at 7:30, Isaac Asimov begins another day at the keyboard. With limited breaks, he types all day, and usually well into the night. He says, "I *must* write. I look upon everything *but* writing as an interruption."

Thanks to over forty years of hard work, Asimov is now among the world's best known and most honored authors. He has written or edited over 300 books and well over a thousand articles, dealing with a wide range of subjects. Very few other writers could come close to matching his number of works, or claim to be experts in so many different fields.

Isaac Asimov's main areas of fame have been science and science fiction. His articles and stories appear monthly in a wide variety of magazines, from *TV Guide* to the magazine that bears his name, *Isaac Asimov's Science Fiction Magazine.*

He has won awards from fans, colleagues, and critics. But perhaps the best proof of Asimov's popularity is this fact: he has sold every story he has written since he turned twenty-one. Throughout his adult years, he has earned a unique place in American writing.

But it was not easy for him to begin his career. As a youngster he had to struggle for the right to just read science fiction magazines. His father sold them in the family candy store, but he refused to let Isaac read "such junk."

"Isaac, you should be reading books with more value," Judah Asimov told him.

"But look at the title of this new magazine," the boy insisted. "It has the word science in it—*Science Wonder Stories*. It has lots of information, and pictures of machines of the future, see? It isn't just junk. Please let me read it for a while."

Isaac Asimov making his acceptance speech for the Hugo Award he received for *The Foundation Trilogy*. The trilogy was named Best Novel Series of All Time in 1966.

Mr. Asimov finally put up his hands in surrender. "All right, Isaac. Take it for a few hours if you must. But don't neglect your library books. I won't have you wasting all your time on trash. That's not why we came to America."

Judah Asimov had brought his family to the United

Isaac's parents, Judah and Anna, in their passport pictures taken in 1922 for the trip to America.

States from Russia in 1923. Isaac was just three years old then, and his sister Marcia was still an infant.

It had not been easy to arrange the departure. Luckily, one of Judah's former classmates helped overcome the complications. Judah had often helped the man with his homework when they were students together. Now, as a government official, the fellow could repay the favor.

Actually, the Asimovs had not been doing badly in Russia. Judah kept the accounts of the family grain mill, and it was still earning a profit. Much of the income came from grinding winter rye, a grain from which the family name had been derived. "Asimov" means "winter son" in Russian, and by 1923 several generations of "winter sons" had lived happily in the town of Petrovichi. Still, Judah and Anna Asimov had decided it was wise to leave their country before life became any tougher there. Anna's half-brother in America urged the family to join him. Judah obtained the passports in Moscow, though he encountered several problems. Finally, in the midst of winter, the family prepared to depart.

On board the *Baltic* they swayed and tossed. Their clothing trunk crashed and banged from one wall of the cabin to another. The Asimovs endured seasickness, horrible food, and considerable anxiety about what the future held in store.

Isaac's family crossed the Atlantic on a liner like these crowded immigrants.

When they finally arrived in America, the family settled in a poor neighborhood of Brooklyn, on the east side of New York City. Judah supported them by taking a series of odd jobs, often in factories.

But when Isaac was in the second grade, his father bought the first of several Asimov candy stores, where he sold newspapers, magazines, cigars, and cigarettes, along with the usual sweets. Judah was much happier being his own boss, even though it meant working very long hours. He tended the store each day from six in the morning until one the next morning. His only real break was from two until four each afternoon, when he took a nap. At this time, no one in the family could make noise or bother him.

The Asimov family lived in a crowded, bustling Brooklyn neighborhood.

From his school days onward, Asimov has always held his audiences spellbound. Here he speaks to a group at the 1981 Lunacon, a science fiction convention.

14

This was also a time when other members of the family had to wait on the customers. Isaac helped his mother and father in the store whenever he was not in school. He even learned to finish his meals as quickly as he could so he could tend the store while someone else ate.

Public School 182 was the first school he attended, but Isaac's education really began before he enrolled there. Isaac taught himself to read when he was five by studying street signs and asking questions of the older children in his neighborhood. When his parents found out that he could read, they proudly helped Isaac develop his new skill. They bought him a dictionary and arranged for him to get a library card.

The library policy of allowing children to check out "just two books at a time" angered Isaac. He read very quickly and this policy meant he had to make the trip to the library every few days. In fact, he read so quickly that each fall when he received his new school books, he finished reading them within a few weeks. He was able to remember almost everything he read, and Asimov's memory is still one of his greatest assets.

Not surprisingly, Isaac was a brilliant student. He advanced through school more quickly than most others. But as long as he stayed in each class, he entertained the other students with his energetically-told jokes and stories from the magazines he read.

Some of his teachers might say that he was *too* entertaining. He was frequently in trouble for talking in class.

He first shared his love of storytelling with his friend "Solly," Solomon Frisch. Solly told Isaac tales of the adventures of "Weapons" Windrows and Jack Winslow, two good guys dedicated to conquering crime. It was the first time Isaac realized that stories did not have to come from books or magazines, that anyone could make up a story.

The boys were seven when Solly spun tales for Isaac, but they soon parted company. Both families moved, and the Asimovs set up housekeeping near Judah's new candy store on Essex Street.

This store was the scene of Isaac's dispute with his father about reading science fiction magazines. He won permission, and from that summer day in 1929 on, he became a devoted fan.

However, science fiction wasn't Isaac's only source of enjoyment. He went to the movies every Saturday and he listened to radio shows like "Little Orphan Annie" or, better yet, "Buck Rogers in the Twenty-Fifth Century." He was a baseball fan, too, and kept his own records of wins and losses and league standings. He puzzled his classmates by rooting for the New York Giants instead of the Brooklyn Dodgers, since he lived in Brooklyn. But he had discovered the

Giants before he knew Brooklyn had its own team, and his loyalty was fixed.

To the other kids, "that brainy Asimov" was often annoying. But they forgave him when he sat in the center of a group at lunchtime, repeating stories from his magazines. He had an almost hypnotic way of describing an adventure.

He loved to please his audience, and he was afraid that someday he would run out of stories. He needed more, and he wished he could own at least some of them for good. He hated returning every magazine to the store rack and every book to the library.

To solve this problem, Isaac first tried copying some of his favorite tales. But this took too much time, and he could only keep a library book for two weeks or a magazine until it was sold from the store. He decided it would be better to write new stories of his own. After all, he had learned from Solly that anyone could make up a story. Now all he had to do was write down what he imagined.

Isaac's first stab at written storytelling was called *The Greenville Chums at College.* It followed a group of hometown buddies on their adventures at the university. Isaac began writing the book just before his twelfth birthday and recorded the first eight chapters in a notebook. Unfortunately, that notebook was lost long ago.

Isaac never finished *The Greenville Chums.* But he did start to take himself seriously as a writer. When he entered high school at twelve years of age, he wrote a column for the school newspaper. That was the first of his work he saw in print.

High school was easy for him, so he was able to graduate when he was only fifteen. That same year, 1935, his father bought Isaac his first typewriter, a used model that cost ten dollars.

Isaac put it to good use. It helped him in his studies at Seth Low Junior College, part of Columbia University. And it helped him prepare letters to the science fiction magazines he was still reading enthusiastically. When he enjoyed a certain story, he praised the author in a letter. If he thought a story was weak, he explained why. His fan letters were his first writing to see print in a science fiction magazine.

Though science fiction greatly interested him, he still considered it just a hobby. Isaac's goal when he entered college was to become a doctor. He needed to study more than he had in high school, so reading and evaluating stories was fit into less spare time.

Still, Isaac took his hobby more and more seriously. In 1936 he began filing his magazines by a special system, carefully making notes about each story. And on May 29, 1937, Isaac Asimov sat down at the typewriter to work on a science fiction story of his

Asimov at fourteen, standing outside the family candy store on Decatur Street where he spent so many hours working.

own, one that he hoped to submit to a favorite magazine. This was the first tale of fiction he invented with the intention of having it published.

The story wasn't finished until the next year. But the completion of his first story was just one of the events that made 1938 a "turning point" year in Asimov's life. Several other important events occurred when he was eighteen, and the diary he had started helped him record them.

On Tuesday, May 10, Isaac noted that his favorite magazine, *Astounding Science Fiction*, did not arrive at the store as expected. He was frantic. He wondered if the magazine had failed under its new editor, John Wood Campbell, Jr.

But he told himself that such a quick loss of faith was foolish. Campbell had always been one of his favorite writers. He had to believe Campbell would be a good leader for the magazine. There must be a simpler reason for the delay.

But Asimov's diary for Wednesday, May 11, grimly stated: "Another day has gone by, and no *Astounding*. I never realized before how much these science fiction magazines mean to me." Isaac spent a hard-earned nickel to call the publishing company, Street & Smith, Inc. A worker there assured him that the magazine was still in business.

He was relieved and waited for nearly another week

John Wood Campbell, Jr., in 1971. He encouraged many other young writers who eventually formed the core of science fiction writing in the 1940s and 1950s. *Astounding Science Fiction* is now titled *Analog Science Fiction/Science Fact.*

to pass. But the next Tuesday's magazine delivery arrived without *Astounding*'s new issue. Now it was May 17, and Isaac decided to take stronger action. He went to the offices of Street & Smith for an explanation.

The subway trip into Manhattan seemed a major expedition to Isaac, for he had only been to that section of New York a few times. Fortunately, he had little trouble finding the building he needed. Gathering all of his courage, he strode into the offices at 79 Seventh Avenue.

An office worker noticed the young man waiting for attention. "I'm Mr. Clifford," he said. "May I help you?"

"Yes, please," Isaac gulped. "Can you tell me when the new issue of *Astounding* will be released?"

"May twentieth," Clifford replied. "That's this coming Friday. We've changed our publication schedule."

"But are you sure? It's already been delayed so long."

"Come, I'll show you the printing dates," Clifford offered. He motioned Isaac toward him and pointed to a large sheet. "See, we've changed things around a bit. But don't worry. We're still going strong."

Isaac felt terrifically relieved. By the time he boarded the subway back to Brooklyn, he knew that he was more serious about science fiction than he had realized.

Now he wanted more than ever to have one of his own stories printed. Though he didn't plan to make writing his profession, he did want to devote more time to it. He pulled his unfinished, year-old story from the drawer and began to work on it again.

On June 19 it was done. Isaac Asimov had completed "Cosmic Corkscrew," a story in which he described time as a spiral that allowed travelers to cross into the future—but only at fixed intervals of several years. Asimov sent his hero on a journey into a time when Earth lay deserted. Because the time intervals were not flexible, the character could not go back just a few days or weeks to find the reason for the disaster. He became more and more frustrated.

Isaac was troubled as he neared the end of his story. He was going to finish it, but would he be able to sell it? Would he fare better by mailing the manuscript in the usual fashion, or by taking it to the magazine office himself?

Judah Asimov offered his advice. "Well, you've taken the subway to Street & Smith once before to ask a question. So why not again? After all, this is a much more important question. And they ought to treat a writer with respect, right? I think you should go see the editor in person."

Isaac was less certain, but he traveled again to the *Astounding* office. "I'd like to see the editor," he said.

Isaac Asimov remained friends with John Campbell until Campbell's death in July 1971. Here Campbell, *left*, talked with Isaac and Isaac's second wife, Janet Jeppson.

The secretary spoke briefly into a telephone, then turned back to him. "Mr. Campbell will see you."

Shaking a little, Isaac entered the editor's office. John Campbell soon set him at ease. He was a large, talkative man who enjoyed discussing ideas with promising writers. He spent over an hour that day with Isaac. He showed him the contents of the next few issues of *Astounding* and told Isaac that another of his letters would appear in the magazine in July.

But what the young writer wanted was to get his *story* into the pages of *Astounding*. Campbell kindly promised to read "Cosmic Corkscrew" that night and send Isaac a letter the next day, even if it were a letter of rejection.

Campbell did turn down the story. But he told Isaac why, and added enough praise to make sure Isaac would keep trying. Isaac didn't waste a day. He immediately started another story.

The writing went much faster this time. By July 18, the author was on his way to Campbell's office again. The editor's enthusiasm was as great as before. Though he also rejected this second story, he continued to fill Isaac with hope for the future. Campbell could tell that Asimov was eager, and that he had talent, though it might take a while to develop.

As Isaac continued writing during the summer of 1938, he tried his luck with a few other editors. When his third story, "Marooned Off Vesta," came back from *Astounding*, he sent it to the editor of *Amazing Stories*. He had confidence in this particular tale, and even though Campbell didn't want it Isaac thought it was good enough to be published. The story was well liked by other members of the Futurian Society, a group of science fiction writers and fans who had just joined forces in New York. Many Futurians who started as fans eventually became successful authors or editors.

On October 21, 1938, Asimov himself joined the ranks of published storytellers: he received a letter from *Amazing*, stating that "Marooned Off Vesta" had been accepted. Ten days later a check arrived to prove it—$64.00 for Asimov's first triumph. Nineteen thirty-eight had been a good year.

Unfortunately, 1939 was less rewarding. Asimov was turned down for medical school admission. Though he wasn't sure he wanted to be a doctor, the letters of rejection were still painful.

Since medical schools would not accept him, Isaac applied for graduate school in chemistry instead. Chemistry was his favorite subject, and he could imagine a fairly happy career as a laboratory scientist. He was admitted for further training at Columbia University.

As he studied for his Master of Arts degree, Asimov continued writing. In fact, during these years he wrote "Nightfall," one of the most highly praised stories of his career. It appeared in *Astounding* in September 1941 and secured a place for Asimov among the "heavyweights" of science fiction. It has repeatedly

Havemeyer Hall at Columbia University in New York, where Isaac worked for his Master of Arts and his Doctorate in chemistry in graduate school.

been voted the best science fiction story of all time, most notably in the 1968-69 poll of the Science Fiction Writers of America and the 1971 poll of the readers of *Analog*.

The setting for "Nightfall" was another planet, where six suns shone instead of our one. Since there

were so many suns, darkness never came—or almost never. Every 2000 years an eclipse occurred, erasing all light. According to the history of this other planet, every "Nightfall" brought panic and madness. Each eclipse caused people to burn everything around them to obtain light.

Above, Isaac at about the time he wrote "Nightfall." *Left*, the cover of the issue of *Astounding* in which "Nightfall" was first published. Isaac was already a popular enough author that his name on the cover meant extra sales for that issue of the magazine.

In "Nightfall" Asimov created characters with varied plans for the next coming period of darkness. For example, scientists and religious leaders were prepared to react quite differently. The conflicts between the various groups became a main focus of the story.

"Nightfall" was an example of Asimov's growing concern with human reactions to scientific events and advances. In literature, this emphasis on technology's impact on people is sometimes called "social science fiction." Asimov is one of its recognized masters.

His "robot stories" fit into this category, too. The first of these, "Robbie," was published in 1940. It featured a mechanical character who acted as nursemaid to a little girl. Like Asimov's other robots, Robbie helped humans rather than harming them. He performed according to Asimov's "Laws of Robotics," which state that robots should protect themselves, but not at the expense of people. Robots are first expected to assist and obey humans.

Asimov put these rules into words with the help of John Campbell. Though Campbell rejected some of Isaac's earliest stories, he published several beginning in 1939. In fact, he supplied the ideas for several of Asimov's best stories. Isaac often discussed story ideas with Campbell, and feels that he owes a debt to Campbell for his patience and encouragement.

Campbell and many other editors watched Asimov's

A robot fan of Isaac's, made by fan George W. Earley. It was bought and presented to Isaac and he keeps it in his office.

fans multiply quickly. In 1941 Isaac sold almost as many stories as in the three previous years combined.

New events were in store in 1942, beginning in February. That Friday the thirteenth was a lucky day, not a jinx, for Asimov: he was accepted by Columbia University for further study in chemistry.

Isaac with his first wife, Gertrude, at the Lunacon science fiction convention in 1968.

Three famous and popular science fiction authors worked together for the Navy in World War II. *Left to right*, L. Sprague de Camp, Robert Heinlein, and Isaac Asimov about 1943.

He would be able to work toward a Ph.D., the highest degree.

The next day, Valentine's Day, Isaac was introduced to a girl named Gertrude Blugerman. He married her less than six months later, and they eventually had two children.

By the time he married, Asimov had interrupted his Ph.D. studies to do research for the U.S. Navy. World

The same three famous and popular science fiction authors (with the addition of Catherine de Camp) at the Science Fiction Writers of America Nebula awards in 1975. *Left to right*, L. Sprague de Camp, Robert Heinlein, Catherine de Camp, and Isaac Asimov.

War II was under way, and the armed forces needed extra scientists. One of Asimov's navy supervisors in Philadelphia was Robert Heinlein, another popular science fiction writer.

Asimov couldn't spend as much time on his stories during the war. And there were times after his return to Ph.D. work when his studies had to come before writing. Still, he managed to move ahead on some major fiction projects in the middle and late 1940s.

Isaac completed his Ph.D. in 1948, and in 1949 he was invited to join the faculty in biochemistry at Boston University Medical School. He was already involved in postdoctoral research at Columbia, but the offer from Boston was more appealing.

In a way, the job in Boston came about from Isaac's writing. He had received a fan letter in 1944 from Professor William Boyd of Boston University Medical School, stating that "Nightfall" was the best story ever printed in *Astounding*. Isaac wrote back, and they had continued to write each other. When a job opened up at the medical school, Boyd offered it to Asimov. Isaac accepted and moved north to Massachusetts with his wife.

In 1950 Dr. William Boyd asked him to help write a textbook. Together they worked on a biochemistry book for medical students. Asimov discovered with pleasure that he could explain science in a very understandable style. He was surprised that the project made him so proud. He realized that he enjoyed nonfiction writing more than lab research, and he hoped that some day he might earn just as much money from it.

His new position combined teaching and research.

Dr. William C. Boyd of Boston University. The textbook he asked Isaac to write with him introduced Isaac to the fun of writing nonfiction.

Asimov quickly became known as one of Boston's liveliest lecturers, delighting his audiences as he had since junior high days. He worked on some interesting problems in the laboratory, too. For a while he was involved in a search for the causes of cancer.

As a new decade began, Isaac Asimov was both a busy chemist and a well-known writer of science fiction. Nearly fifty of his stories had been published, and his first novel, *Pebble in the Sky*, was in print. His career now began to expand quickly into other areas.

The photograph of Isaac Asimov which appeared on the cover
of *Pebble in the Sky*. Isaac thought it made him look like a
movie star and wanted to keep it on all of his books. His wife
Gertrude advised against it.

The Asimov family in 1965: Isaac's daughter Robyn, his son David, Gertrude and Isaac. Asimov had begun writing the Lucky Starr series for children about the time he became a father.

However, when Asimov turned to writing science nonfiction, he didn't leave fiction behind. In fact, he began to produce a wider range of fiction than before. In 1953 he sold a science fiction novel for children, the first in a series about the hero Lucky Starr. Asimov wrote the series under a "pen name," Paul French. Most characters besides the hero changed from book to book, but a few appeared more than once.

Throughout the 1950s Asimov kept pounding away at the typewriter in his workroom. The number of his published books and shorter works rose steadily.

Asimov is still a proud father and embarrasses his daughter Robyn with compliments whenever he can.

Readers and critics raved especially about three books known as *The Foundation Trilogy,* the last of which appeared in 1953. (Asimov went back to the series in 1982 and has since added more books to it.)

Isaac holding up the base of the Hugo he won for Best Novel for *The Gods Themselves*. The spaceship which goes on the base *(see photograph on page 8)* was added later.

The series contained nine stories about the break-up of the Galactic Empire. Today the idea of space kingdoms is a familiar one. But when Asimov's *Foundation* books were published, they marked a new trend. And though the collapse of an empire may sound quite violent, the books actually focused more on politics than on warfare. Not every fan and critic agreed with the ideas behind Asimov's stories, but nearly all did agree that the series was a high-quality achievement. Asimov's reputation was now even more secure.

Based on the growing acclaim for his writing, Asimov became more confident about succeeding as a full-time author. In 1958 he told his wife that he would like to leave teaching and make writing his primary profession.

"But what will we live on?" she asked.

"The books," he answered, sure that he could make a living from them. His decision was firm.

He left his job as a professor and began producing more books, stories, and articles than ever. He also began to cover a wider range of topics than ever. More and more readers became familiar with his name.

Asimov wrote joke books, murder mysteries, and explanations of history. He helped readers understand Shakespeare and the Bible. And he took pleasure in explaining the origins of words. *Clone, robot,* and

Isaac Asimov can pose beside an entire bookcase full of books by him. This was taken in his New York apartment in 1976, and he has added many books to his shelves since then.

laser are just a few of the terms he tracked down in the book *More Words of Science.*

In his writing, Dr. Asimov used his vast knowledge to reflect upon the state of the world and its future.

He first warned of a world population boom and energy crisis many years ago. Now these problems are acknowledged by more people, but Dr. Asimov is afraid they will not be solved soon enough. He fears that "Five hundred years from now a survived civilization will talk about the Dark Ages of the twenty-first century."

Autographing books for a fan at a convention in Washington, D.C., in 1981.

Despite his pessimism, Asimov willingly shares his advice on the human present and future. He often appears on television, as an expert on everything from computers to solar power to space exploration. He is also asked to write magazine articles, for publications too numerous to list.

Isaac Asimov on "The Mike Douglas Show" with *(left)* Mike Douglas and *(right)* actor Robert Stack in 1973. As always, he was an amusing and entertaining speaker.

Asimov's dedication and hard work have produced shelves of books under his name. Here he is working in part of his library in his New York apartment.

Asimov can get it all done because he works with intensity and dedication, worrying and hurrying constantly. In a way, he feels that he is still proving to his father that he isn't lazy. "I am forever and always in the candy store, and the work must be done," he wrote in the first book of his autobiography, *In Memory Yet Green* (Doubleday, 1979). "The memory of my father is with me constantly and it is that, more than anything else, that has made me so prolific."

Amazingly, Asimov works without assistance. He has no secretary and no researchers. He does all his typing and answers all his fan letters himself. It is little wonder, then, that his work days are long.

Of course, there are interruptions, but no more than necessary. On the rare occasions when he wants to take a break, Asimov might watch TV, read, or talk to his second wife, Janet Jeppson. He married her in 1973 after divorcing his first wife.

He takes as few vacations as possible. There are out-of-town speaking trips, since Asimov is among the nation's most desired lecturers. And even en route, he writes, in longhand if he must. When he returns to his typewriter in New York, Dr. Asimov is truly back in his favorite place. He is a writer by choice, and he chooses to write even on weekends and holidays.

He rattles the keyboard at the pace of 90 words a minute, producing thousands of words each day. The first draft is still written on a typewriter, but then Isaac enters each page onto a word processor, rewriting as he types. If an editor requests, he will revise a project, but only once. Often there are few changes from the first draft.

A proud Isaac holding one of his Nebula Awards, the one he received for *The Gods Themselves* as Best Novel. The Nebula is given by the Science Fiction Writers of America.

As soon as Asimov completes one project, he is engulfed in another. In 1981, he returned to science fiction and has since written four novels: *Foundation's Edge*, *Robots of Dawn*, *Robots and Empire*, and *Foundation and Earth*. All have been best-sellers. He

Isaac with his second wife, Janet, in 1975.

Two of Isaac's Nebula awards. Each award is handmade and therefore different from every other. The one on the right shows a problem Isaac has met all his life—no one can spell his name!

Isaac Asimov in 1986. He shows the strain of his coronary in 1977 and his more recent heart surgery.

has two more novels under contract, is working on a book on subatomic particles and on an annotation of the Gilbert & Sullivan operettas. Isaac Asimov has published 340 books so far. He has already written more books about a greater number of subjects than any other author in America.

He has won many prizes for his efforts, but he is reluctant to list them all. He prefers to acknowledge just his five Hugo Awards and two Nebula Awards. Each of these signified a high distinction in science fiction. Asimov is especially proud of the 1966 Hugo which named *The Foundation Trilogy* as Best Novel Series of All Time. More recently, *The Gods Themselves* and *The Bicentennial Man* both received the Hugo and Nebula awards the year of their publication.

Isaac Asimov has been adding to our supply of knowledge and entertainment for over forty years, and he's still going strong. One writer has called him "the human writing machine," a nickname he has certainly earned. But astronomer Carl Sagan has given him a more meaningful title. Sagan says Asimov is "the great explainer of the age." That's an accurate description of this unique man—a writer and scientist who has shown us many sides of our past, present, and future.

BIBLIOGRAPHY

If you were to look in the list of BOOKS IN PRINT for Isaac Asimov's works, you would find over a page and a half of titles in very small type. Below are a few of Isaac Asimov's works for children.

On the subject of science:

Alpha Centauri, the Nearest Star. New York: Lothrop, Lee & Shepard, 1976. Illustrated, for grades 7 and up.

The Clock We Live On. New York: Harper & Row, 1965. Illustrated, for grades 7 and up.

Environments Out There. New York: Harper & Row, 1967. Illustrated, for grades 5 through 10.

How Did We Find Out About Dinosaurs? New York: Walker & Co., 1981. Illustrated, for grades 5 through 8.

The Human Body. Boston: Houghton Mifflin, 1963. Illustrated, for grades 7 and up.

Inside The Atom. New York: Harper & Row, 1974. Illustrated, for grades 7 and up.

The Realm of Measure. Boston: Houghton Mifflin, 1961. Illustrated, for grades 7 and up.

Satellites In Outer Space. New York: Random House, 1964. Illustrated, for grades 3 through 5.

What Makes The Sun Shine? Boston: Little, Brown, 1971. Illustrated, for grades 4 through 6.

On the subject of history:

The Birth of the United States. Boston: Houghton Mifflin, 1974. Illustrated, for grades 7 and up.

The Dark Ages. Boston: Houghton Mifflin, 1968. With maps, for grades 7 and up.

Greeks: A Great Adventure. Boston: Houghton Mifflin, 1965. Illustrated, for grades 7 and up.

Land of Canaan. Boston: Houghton Mifflin. Illustrated, for grades 7 and up.

The Shaping of North America. Boston: Houghton Mifflin, 1973. Illustrated, for grades 7 through 12.

On the subject of language:

Words from the Myths. Boston: Houghton Mifflin, 1961. Illustrated, for grades 5 through 10.

Words of Science. Boston: Houghton Mifflin, 1959. Illustrated, for grades 7 and up.

Words on the Map. Boston: Houghton Mifflin, 1962. Illustrated, for grades 7 and up.

Fiction and other writing:

Animals of the Bible. New York: Doubleday, 1978. Illustrated, for grades 2 through 5.

Great Ideas of Science. Boston: Houghton Mifflin, 1969. Illustrated, for grades 7 and up.

The Key Word & Other Mysteries. New York: Avon, 1979. Illustrated, for grades 2 through 6.

Lucky Starr & The Big Sun of Mercury. New York: Fawcett, 1978.

Books Asimov wrote or edited with other people:

Hallucination Orbit: Psychology in Science Fiction. New York: Farrar, Straus & Giroux, 1983. Grades 3 through 6.

After the End. Milwaukee, WI: Raintree Publishers, 1981. Illustrated science fiction, for grades 5 through 7.

Earth Invaded. Milwaukee, WI: Raintree Publishers, 1982. Illustrated science fiction, for grades 5 through 7.

Fantastic Creatures. Milwaukee, WI: Raintree Publishers, 1981. Science fiction, for grades 7 and up.

Tomorrow's TV. Milwaukee, WI: Raintree Publishers, 1982. Illustrated science fiction, for grades 5 through 7.

Norby, the Mixed-Up Robot. Written with Janet Asimov. New York: Walker & Co., 1983. Science fiction, for grades 5 through 7.

Asimov's Awards
<u>for Science Fiction</u>

The Science Fiction Achievement Award
(the Hugo)

These awards are chosen by vote of
everyone who attends the annual
World Science Fiction Convention

1963   Special Award for Distinguished Contribution
to the Field of Science Fiction

1966   *The Foundation Trilogy*   Best Novel Series
of All Time
1973   *The Gods Themselves*   Best Novel
1977   "The Bicentennial Man"   Best Novelette
1983   *Foundation's Edge*   Best Novel

The Nebula Award

These awards are chosen annually by the members
of the Science Fiction Writers of America

1973   *The Gods Themselves*   Best Novel
1976   "The Bicentennial Man"   Best Novella

ACKNOWLEDGEMENTS

Photos courtesy of: Boston University Medical Center, p. 36, photo by Bradford Herzog, p. 2; Library of Congress, p. 12; Community Service Society, p. 13; Columbia University, p. 27. Photos by Jay Kay Klein, pp. 1, 6, 8, 14, 21, 24, 31, 32, 33, 34, 38, 39, 40, 42, 43, 45, 47, 48, 49, 50.

Illustration p. 44 from IN JOY STILL FELT by Isaac Asimov. Copyright © 1980 by Isaac Asimov. Reprinted by permission of Doubleday & Company, Inc.

Illustrations pp. 10, 19, 29, 37 from IN MEMORY YET GREEN by Isaac Asimov. Copyright © 1979 by Isaac Asimov. Reprinted by permission of Doubleday & Company, Inc.

Jacket p. 28 from *Astounding Science Fiction*, copyright 1941 by Street & Smith Publications, Inc.; renewed © 1968 by Condé Nast Publications, Inc. Reproduced by permission of Davis Publications, Inc.

Front cover photograph by Jay Kay Klein. Back cover photograph by Bradford Herzog, Boston University Medical Center.